Hyper-Grace

THE DANGEROUS DOCTRINE
OF A HAPPY GOD

D. R. Silva

Up-Arrow Publishing
Havre, Montana

Contents

Introduction 1

Is "Hyper-Grace" Biblical? 9

The Problem with "Grace" 21

Are You Saying All Sins Are Forgiven? 33

Are You Saying Repentance Isn't Necessary? 49

Are You Saying We Can Sin All We Want? 61

Concluding Remarks 69

Other Books by D. R. Silva 75

To everyone who has suffered loss for the sake of the gospel.
May we never lose heart; may we never sell out.

"Using words like 'extreme' and 'hyper' in order to insult the message of grace, is like attempting to insult light by calling it 'illuminating,' or water by calling it 'wet.' Yes, Grace is both extreme and hyper...would you rather it be 'moderate' and 'docile'?"

— *Jeff Turner*

Introduction

In February 2013, Michael Brown put out an article confronting the errors he has perceived in the "modern grace message." In it he coined the term "hyper-grace." Since then, the term has quickly become another slanderous word in Charismatic circles, being naively thrown around by people who are trying to write-off a message they've never actually looked into for themselves.

It's clear by the way people talk, that the only thing that makes them think this message is "bad," is that some popular church leaders said it is. This is evidenced by the fact that many of the people filling their Facebook and Twitter pages with slander against "hyper-grace" teachers are only repeating what the leaders have assumed this message is saying.

During my time as part of this "grace movement," I've encountered hundreds of people who have come up with (or repeated) different terms used to insult the grace message (Dr. Brown certainly isn't the first), yet every time the accusations start flying, they can always be summed up to one fear: "Grace is not a license to sin!" The problem with this "hyper-grace" label is that it comes with many presumptions and false accusations—none of which are ever accompanied by any evidence. But even with a lack of evidence, the accusers of this movement still insist that we are saying people should run around and sin, repentance isn't needed, confession is stupid, and many other presumptuous claims. Worse yet, others who read those accusations naively buy into them and repeat those things to others.

Many of the sheep in the church have been primed for this moment. Buzzwords like "honor" and "submission" have been thrown around and subtly repeated over the years to coerce the flock into agreeing with whatever the leaders preach. To disagree or challenge a leader's stance is seen as "dishonoring" and "unsubmissive." I've seen some pastors influenced by those words go so far as saying that unless you submit to your pastor (them) you cannot experience God's blessings. The blatant manipulation should be obvious, but because these twisted definitions of "honor" and "submission" have been so engrained in the sheep, the congregation just gives a faithful "amen!" to their mental slavery without hesitation.

As a result of this common blind obedience, the flock never checks into "controversies" like "hyper-grace" for themselves and they only swallow whatever their leader feeds them. Biased articles appear on Charismatic Christian websites, reeking of religious propaganda, false witness, and blatant lies, but the people just buy into it, hook, line and sinker. Followers have been trained to do what they're told without argument, and without daring to think for themselves. If anyone does dare to challenge popular ideas, others come along and try to bully that person back into line, insinuating the person with questions isn't being faithful to God, or they are "bashing" other believers, or even "touching the Lord's anointed!"

A common tactic is to throw a negative label on the other person's idea to diminish their voice, and hopefully shame them enough to recant or at the very least cause others to reject them so their ideas don't spread. All it takes is for one popular leader to scream "heresy!" and the congregation will be up in arms with pitchforks and torches held high! Someone who was a "brother" to the congregation last Sunday instantly becomes a "lost soul" in need of our gossipy prayers.

Through the years, whenever I've challenged the stances of popular leaders, I've had many followers of that leader accuse me of attacking the person. These accusers never addresses or acknowledge the points and scriptures I've brought up in defense of my position, they simply conclude that because I'm challenging this leader's teaching, I'm attacking the leader as a person—"Don't touch the Lord's anointed!" they yell. And in their minds, that's a good enough excuse to ignore all the evidence and walk away feeling even more reassured in their blind loyalty. John G. Lake called that kind of behavior "inordinate affection," and it's absolutely out of control in the American church.[1]

We don't mind screaming "heretic!" at Joel Osteen for insinuating God actually wants us to enjoy our lives on Earth, but don't you dare infer that *my* pastor might be teaching something unbiblical. *OH, no!* That's simply incomprehensible! Everything preached by *my* pastor is "the word of the Lord," he told me so! And since he tells me before each sermon that it's "the word of the Lord," my right to question and disagree is completely void, since if I decide to voice any opposition or opinion contrary to his, I'm immediately seen as being argumentative with the Lord.

How then, can anybody ever look into "hyper-grace" and judge it fairly when the leaders are putting such negative labels on it in an attempt to scare others away? If anybody does ever try to look into "hyper-grace" on their own, they can only do so with the negative filter they've been given by their leaders. They've already been taught to view the message and the teachers with prejudice, so they'll be unable to view it any differently. Their minds have been programmed to see only what their leaders have told them to see.

Despite the fact that Paul told the church to "Test everything and hold on to the good," many Christians today let their leaders test everything for them, and just take their word for the results they bring back. They aren't taught to find manipulation and deception on their own, they're only told what and where it is, and warned to stay away. Consequently, the leaders have full control over what gets labeled deception (anything that goes against their beliefs) and what gets a free pass (anything that serves to promote their beliefs). It's really quite backwards from scripture, and it's nothing more than religious manipulation and bullying under the guise of spirituality—it's an abuse of authority.

A good teacher doesn't expect you to blindly obey everything they teach. A good teacher teaches you how to do research and study for yourself, to see if what they are saying holds true. There are a lot of good speakers nowadays, but very few good teachers.

✳✳✳

Although I don't like being lumped into categories like "hyper-grace" or "grace movement," I understand that if my beliefs were to be lumped into any category at this time in my life, they would fit into what has been labeled "hyper-grace." Therefore I think it's fair for me to provide a perspective as someone on the "inside," for those who claim to be seeking "balance," rather than leaving the argument one-sided, coming from a person who has never spent time in or among this "movement," isn't personal friends with any of the "key teachers," and has only read a few books on the subject and drawn conclusions from those.

In this book, I want to explain what I personally believe about grace, how I've interpreted this "hyper-grace" message over the years, and provide you with clarity as to what is and isn't actually being said within this "movement." I think most of what Dr. Brown,

Mike Bickle and all of their loyal followers are opposing is only based on what they've read into the message through their own misinterpretation or misuse of our message.

I find it strange, that even with the abundant lack of evidence, these accusations and assumptions have continued to be passed off as "facts." Although many over the years have come to us with the same accusations and have put the same words in our mouths about giving people a license to sin, hating holiness, and saying repentance is ridiculous, nobody in the grace camp has actually ever said those things at all, and none of the accusers ever seem to have any reference for where anyone has, but they will sure insist that it's happening *all over.*

Note that my intention with this book isn't to debate or return slander with slander. I want to see the church united, and I have no agenda to drive it apart any further than it is. As I read more of Dr. Brown's articles and comments concerning this issue, I think it's safe to conclude that he wants the same, though I'm also convinced that he doesn't truly understand this message. My only intention here is to give you a clear perspective of what people in this "movement" are actually trying to get across, and why it comes off as such a threat.

If Dr. Brown happens to read this, let me say thank you for doing what you think needs to be done in order to protect your flock and help move the church forward. I'm confident that your heart is not to stir up debates and arguments for the sake of flaunting your Bible knowledge or causing controversy, but that you do have a true desire to see the church living up to her full potential in Jesus—whatever you think that looks like. This is something we have in common, and I hope we will find it as a point to come together, not move apart. Though I disagree with most of what I've seen you and Mr.

Bickle teaching on this subject, I still consider you my brothers, not my enemies. In that, I hope you read this book like a response in a conversation, not as an attack on your character. I only wish to provide my perspective of this matter, just as you have in your book and articles.

I'm not writing this to respond to the points made in Dr. Brown's book, but to respond to the overall arguments being made against this movement by those who have naively bought into the slanderous claims that have been made. Many of those claims have originated, or been influenced by Dr. Brown's stance on this issue, but again, this is not meant to be a direct response to his book.

***

Let me also note that through the years, I've known people who have attempted to dialogue with Mike Bickle, Lou Engle, and other popular Charismatic leaders about these issues (before they ever became as big as they are now), but those people were promptly ignored, turned away, or told to pack up and leave their churches. Those in smaller churches have found similar results. So let the reader be aware that a large portion of this "grace movement" isn't a result of rebellion or "lack of honor" for leadership, but a lack of communication and responsibility on the side of the leaders, and oftentimes a blatant refusal to answer questions and address the glaring issues and contradictions in the popular traditions of the church's modern teachings.

If our leaders aren't willing to provide us with satisfying answers that point to Jesus, and they avoid any questions we have about Him and where He is in most of our modern Christian traditions, then we must obey our conscience and do what needs to be done to find those answers on our own. For many, this has meant leaving or being kicked out of their church, losing friends, homes, cars, families, jobs, ministry positions, and much more. We haven't suffered these things because we want to rebel or live lawless lives, but because we want the person (not the tradition) of Jesus. And through all of the seeking we were told to do, and the endless promises of revival on the horizon, we never found Him in our churches. We did what we needed to do for the sake of our relationship with Him. We didn't "forsake the fellowship," we took the necessary measures needed to go out and find it.

I don't say any of that to stir up bad feelings towards any church leaders, but to let the reader know that many in the "grace camp" have reached out to our leaders with questions and concerns, but many of those leaders haven't been willing to address those things, and it seems the only reason they're deciding to now is because the waves we've caused in their congregations have become too big to be ignored any longer.

✳✳✳

I write this, not with the hope of proving anybody wrong, but with the hope of continuing this conversation on Grace, and giving a clear presentation of this message. One of my greatest hopes as a Christian is that the church as a whole will actually sit down and talk about our disagreements in a way where we aren't turning our respective "groups" against each other, or taking cheap-shots at people to diminish their value and their voice. Even more, I hope that we will abandon this need to drive everything into "camps" and categories with the intention of using our armies to debate and demonize those we disagree with. Instead let us once again accept, just as the early apostles did, that there is only one category that we are all included in: Christ (Gal. 3:28).

As I remind all of my readers: look into these things for yourself. Don't only take Dr. Brown's word for it, and don't only take my word for it. Seek answers and truth for yourself ("test everything and hold onto what is good"). Every church leader is capable of leading people astray (intentionally or not), whether a self-published author or a PhD.

We are not the mediators between you and God, Jesus is. He lives in you as much as He lives in us. You have the same spirit we do, and you are anointed by the same Anointed One as we are. Different degrees of influence don't equate to different degrees of spirituality. We are all on the same level. Although pastors are great for leading, they are not meant to be your theological babysitters for your whole life. At some point, if you really want to thrive in your Christian life, you need to learn how to feed yourself.

The internet is your endless universe of learning resources. You can practically Google search anything these days and it will come up for free. There are online concordances, dictionaries, etymologies, genealogies, and pretty much anything you can think of. We're past the days of $100,000 degrees, and everything you need is right within your reach. If you really want to keep yourself from being deceived, take advantage of this privilege and educate yourself. Don't merely settle for books that promise to keep you from deception, those are sometimes the most deceiving ones.

Endnotes

[1] A version of "God's Love vs. Inordinate Affection, by John G. Lake" can be found on my website at SaintsNotSinners.org.

CHAPTER 1

Is "Hyper-Grace" Biblical?

Let me start this out by saying that this idea that there's a group of people running around telling others that it's okay to sin is ridiculous! The worst years of my life were spent as a Christian stuck in sin, taught by my leaders that I was prone to live that way until I died. I would never even think of giving Christians a reason to live that hell. This is such an insulting accusation, and the people making these claims have no evidence of it. If anything is a license to sin, it's the popular idea that it's your nature to do it. The grace message, on the other hand, teaches that the sinful nature was removed and you are now free to live a life of righteousness and purity away from the burden of force and obligation.

After spending four years among the "grace movement," and countless hours talking to people, reading their Facebook posts, watching their YouTube videos, and scrolling their blogs, I've never once seen or heard a single person say that it's okay to sin because we have grace. Yet, opponents of "hyper-grace" throw this accusation around as if there are thousands of people saying these kinds of things, when nobody is at all!

There are numerous people within the "grace camp" whose interpretations of grace I disagree with, but not even they are saying the silly things people are claiming. If there is anyone doing that as blatantly as people are making it seem, then their voice hasn't ever become big enough to be noticed or to spread. If it had, I guarantee that a lot of people in the "grace camp" wouldn't have hesitated to voice their disagreements.

Many of us are lifelong Christians who spent most of our church lives trapped in sin. We were miserable and hated our lives because we wanted to do good but [thought] we had no power to do it. The message of Grace and God's absolute kindness and happiness with us is what really set us free. It didn't make us want to look for excuses to continue in that hell we were in, but instead it empowered us to leave.

What's On the Inside?

It seems today, that any person who says God is happy and not concerned with the rules is automatically accused and slandered by those who think God is angry and bringing harsh judgment down on the heads of "sinners." This message of God's happiness is often misinterpreted as saying, "Go break all the rules and sin all you want! Have an orgy on the church altar! God doesn't care, He's happy!" This is nothing more than pure slander, and it isn't based on anything anyone in the "grace camp" is actually saying.

To the rule-focused person, rules and outward appearances are the most important thing. And when they aren't emphasized over grace and kindness, the person concludes that the teacher must be a wishy-washy heretic who is "soft on sin." Joel Osteen is still being gossiped about on the front pages of Charismatic websites, criticized because he chooses not to condemn homosexuals. The very fact that I just mentioned Joel Osteen in a non-condemning way has given some people reading this the impression that I must be a devoted supporter of him and what he teaches, since if I wasn't, surely I would have mentioned him in negative light! And the people who think with this kind of logic are the ones claiming to have the true understanding of "grace." There is nothing graceful about that kind of thinking.

The logic is often that if you're not preaching hard Law and judging sinners and condemning their sin (which often ends up being us condemning the people instead), or if you're not using the Law to coerce believers into living holy and pure, than you must be a false teacher! Why is this so often the only conclusion presented? This idea that the Law needs to be emphasized more than grace is a deception in itself since most of Paul's letters were written to warn Christians *not* to go running back to Laws and rule-keeping as a means of righteousness and purity. Read Galatians 3 for a clear example. Or even better, read Galatians 5 where he gets so frustrated with the teachers who are dragging people back into Law-keeping that he says he wishes they would just go the whole way with their religion and castrate themselves! Does it sound like he was trying to enforce the Law so people would live pure? Hardly.

> *"If with Christ you died to the elemental spirits of the world, why, as if you were still alive in the world, do you submit to regulations— "Do not handle, Do not taste, Do not touch" (referring to things that all perish as they are used)—according to human precepts and teachings? These have indeed an appearance of wisdom in promoting self-made religion and asceticism and severity to the body, but they are of no value in stopping the indulgence of the flesh." – Col. 2:20-21 (ESV)*

God isn't concerned with the rules—the keeping of which is only an outside display of goodness that only better serves to boost the religious ego—He's concerned with the hearts of people. Those rules, no matter how many you keep, can never change your heart. God is interested in your heart, not your appearance (don't we quote that verse all the time?).[1]

Jesus called the Pharisees whitewashed tombs and said they looked great on the outside, but inside they were full of dead men's bones. Once again, He's concerned with the inside. Or how about when He said, "wash the inside of the cup and the outside of the cup will also be cleaned"? You can scrub the outside of the cup until it shines like gold and impresses everyone around you with its splendor, and the inside (which is the place that really matters) can still be full of mold. But change the perspective of your heart (clean the inside of the cup) and the behavior (the outside of the cup) will change accordingly, without the weight of burdens and obligation.

This is the message of grace being preached. Not that you don't need to turn away from your sin, but that when you turn to God and keep your focus on the cross and the work of Christ, sin is turned away from as a natural result, without it needing to be your main priority.

My focus isn't on changing my behavior, but on changing my perspective to match His. In the changing of my perspective (to see what He has already done and who He is in me), my behavior changes naturally without me having to work it up through rigorous self-discipline and religious rituals that never work.

✳✳✳

People love to criticize the "grace movement" and say we're telling people that "works" don't mean anything. They say, "Faith without works is dead!" Yes. And works without faith are just as dead. Faith results in works, but works never result in faith. The works that result from faith aren't coming from strenuous efforts to get anything out of God or impress Him with your performance, but from the peace and rest that comes from knowing He has already given you everything you need.[2] It's the result of a changed perspective not harder labor. If you're trying to keep the Law, you're not in faith. "The Law is not based on faith." (Gal. 3:12)

The foundation of this so-called "hyper-grace" message is that we are free to rest from our religious efforts. We're not under obligation to keep the standards of the old, but instead we're under the grace of God who gives freely based on His ability to love, not our ability to earn His love through our good behavior. Does that make us want to be lazy? If it did, "hyper-grace" wouldn't be the hot topic of conversation that it is, since none of us would have felt the need to spend so many hours preaching this gospel to people and setting them free. We would have just accepted that God is pleased with us and laid down in our beds for the rest our lives, listening to Godfrey Birtill and giggling our little heads off. No. This rest doesn't make us lazy, it makes us at peace with God and ourselves because we know He has settled every sin issue for us. Now we can throw our hands in the air and say, "I believe!" Our works don't come from a pressure to please God, but from the peace of the promise that He is already pleased.

Where is "Hyper-Grace" in Scripture?

Though I despise how this "hyper-grace" label has been used by the opponents of this message, and I think it only gives people another reason to throw stones at those they deem heretics, "hyper-grace" is actually used in scripture as a positive reinforcement of God's grace over sin. No, "hyper-grace" preachers haven't created their own weird Bible translation just for this point, you can actually look it up in your own Bible and it will say the same thing.

Hyperperisseuō (ὑπερπερισσεύω) is the word Paul used in Romans 5:20 to say "grace abounds over sin."[3] It comes from two root words:

1. Huper[4] (ὑπέρ) (where we get our English word "hyper"), AND
2. Perisseuō[5] (περισσεύω) (where we get our English word "abound").

So while many are running around saying "hyper-grace" is a "deception" (or even the "great deception of the 21st century"), "hyper-grace" is actually a concept in scripture, and Paul was technically a "hyper-grace" preacher (in fact, he would have been the first one).

The transliteration of Romans 5:20 would read, "Where sin abounds, grace hyper-abounds." Does it mean you can run around sinning? No. Read the very next verse.

> "What shall we say, then? Shall we go on sinning so that grace may increase? By no means! We are those who have died to sin; how can we live in it any longer?" – Romans 6:1-2 (NIV)

While scripture says grace abounds over sin (where sin flows, grace overflows), Paul also immediately includes the necessary disclaimer (to avoid the obvious accusations we're now receiving), that this doesn't mean we can go around sinning. Then he goes into Romans 6 explaining that we're completely free from sin.

If you build your sin to the sky, God has already built His grace for you to the moon. If you then build your sin to the moon, He has already built His grace to the Sun. Grace will *always* be a thousand steps ahead of your sin. (Paul seemed to think this was *good* news.) Is it a reason to sin, that you should find grace built up to the Sun? No! Paul immediately answers the question they're all thinking, "Should we continue in sin to get more grace? God forbid! We are those who have been freed from sin. How can we continue living in it?"

Then, not only is "hyper-grace" in scripture, but it's used in a positive way to reinforce the goodness of the Gospel of God's grace.

Yet, today it's being used in a *negative* way to slander the message of grace and the people who teach it, causing others to dismiss this message as unbiblical heresy and cling to their precious rulebooks and traditions harder than ever before.

So who is really being deceived here? Those who subscribe to this "hyper-grace" message (one that Paul also preached)? Or those who are being told that this kind of grace is a deception they need to stay away from? If it's true that "hyper-grace" is a deception, then Paul has deceived billions of Christians through church history by writing about that kind of grace in scripture. Not only that, but Dr. Brown and others would be in error by calling this "the deception of the 21st century," since this deception has existed in scripture for the past 20 centuries, ever since those letters were written.

Despite the fact that we teach these things clearly (even giving the same disclaimers Paul gave), many will still accuse us of "condoning sin," and telling people to run around and do whatever they want. It's a false accusation and slander, nothing more. And yet, these false accusations are also nothing new.

"License to Sin" Accusations against Paul

Since Paul emphasized God's grace and kindness abounding over sin rather than strict Laws and harsh judgment, he got the same accusations that many in this "hyper-grace" movement are receiving.

"It's simply perverse to say, 'If my lies serve to show off God's truth all the more gloriously, why blame me? I'm doing God a favor.' Some people are actually trying to put such words in our mouths, claiming that we go around saying, 'The more evil we do, the more good God does, so let's just do it!' That's pure slander, as I'm sure you'll agree." – Romans 3:8 (MESSAGE)

"So what do we do? Keep on sinning so God can keep on forgiving? I should hope not! If we've left the country where sin is sovereign, how can we still live

> *in our old house there? Or didn't you realize we packed up and left there for*
> *good? That is what happened in baptism. When we went under the water, we*
> *left the old country of sin behind; when we came up out of the water, we*
> *entered into the new country of grace—a new life in a new land!" – Romans*
> *6:1-2 (MESSAGE)*

> *So, since we're out from under the old tyranny, does that mean we can live*
> *any old way we want? Since we're free in the freedom of God, can we do*
> *anything that comes to mind? Hardly. You know well enough from your own*
> *experience that there are some acts of so-called freedom that destroy freedom.*
> *Offer yourselves to sin, for instance, and it's your last free act. But offer*
> *yourselves to the ways of God and the freedom never quits. All your lives*
> *you've let sin tell you what to do. But thank God you've started listening to a*
> *new master, one whose commands set you free to live openly in his freedom!*
> *– Romans 6:15 (MESSAGE)*

Note that he wasn't actually saying any of those things about going around and sinning, but people were still putting those words in his mouth in order to slander him and discredit his message. He agreed with the accusers that "grace isn't a license to sin," but he was never saying it was to begin with, *they were!*

This is the same exact thing that's going on now. Nobody has actually ever said "grace is a license to sin," but these opponents of grace have put those words in people's mouths and used these myths to demonize the teachers in front of their congregations, causing the congregations to reject the entire message (and of course, the messengers along with it).

If a great deception is lurking anywhere in the church, it's in this counter-argument to the grace message that's completely based on lies and misconceptions that are being passed off as truth and facts. By definition then, if you believe what you've heard from these anti-"hyper-grace" teachers without ever looking into it for yourself, then it's you who have been deceived by them.

Deceive[6] — to cause to believe what is not true; mislead.

Is "Hyper-Grace" Logical?

The interesting thing about this opposition to "hyper-grace," is that the word "hyper" means "extremely active." Therefore, the term "hyper-grace" actually means "extremely active grace." So by even coming up with a term like "hyper-grace" and using it in a negative way, what you are saying is that you would much more prefer a less active grace—you're offended by how active we're making grace seem.

Look at this list I've compiled of some of the synonyms of the word hyper. For fun, I'll add the word "grace" after each one just so you can get an idea of what the term "hyper-grace" actually implies (and consequently, what people are really opposing).

Synonyms of Hyper:[7]

Alive-Grace

Bold-Grace

Busy-Grace

Determined-Grace

Diligent-Grace

Dynamic-Grace

Eager-Grace

Energetic-Grace

Engaged-Grace

Enthusiastic-Grace

Intense-Grace

Lively-Grace

Ready-Grace

Daring-Grace

Purposeful-Grace

Zealous-Grace

Which of the above do you have a problem with?

People say, "We need to get rid of 'hyper-grace'!" So then what do you want, the opposite? Because here's what those are:

Antonyms of Hyper:

Afraid-Grace

Apathetic-Grace

Cowardly-Grace

Dull-Grace

Idle-Grace

Ignorant-Grace

Inactive-Grace

Lazy-Grace

Lifeless-Grace

Stupid-Grace

Uneducated-Grace

Unenthusiastic-Grace

Weak-Grace

Dormant-Grace

Immobile-Grace

Which of those "graces" do you fancy most?

Study to Show Yourself Approved

I'm not even pointing all that out as a means to convince you to embrace the term "hyper-grace" (though it does make me more interested in it!), I'm merely trying to encourage you to actually educate yourself, do your own research, and find out what people are really saying before you jump on the bandwagon, flocking to the latest protest based on the latest trendy label to oppose.

Don't be naive enough to think "hyper-grace" is the last term that will come out and be promoted as a "great deception." As soon people find opportunity to create another controversy that sells books and gets clicks on their blog page, they'll make up another label for it and start opposing that as well. Call it "strange fire," "hyper-grace," "word of faith," it doesn't matter; this nonsense has been going on for thousands of years.

Don't just read the Bible! Read a dictionary, a thesaurus, a concordance, and whatever else you can get your hands on. It doesn't matter how many books you read promising to expose the latest "great deception," if you don't have the capacity to think and reason for yourself, you'll still find yourself deceived because you have no choice but to believe whatever that person is telling you.

Check the references in the back of this book, I'm not only providing them for the sake of backing my case, but for the sake of giving you a starting point to do your own investigations and research. I don't want you to read what I write here and think, "He makes a great point, therefore I'm going to say 'amen' and believe him!" No. I don't want to recreate the religious system I escaped from. I don't want to be your new pulpit preacher, dragging you out of someone else's belief system and into mine. I want to teach you how to think. I want to teach you how to test and examine what you're told. I want to teach you how to ask questions. Because if you rely on me to give you all the answers and I disappear tomorrow, you will be helpless and lost, like so many in the church become when their favorite leader falls.

Until proven otherwise, assume that I'm out to get you, and test everything I say to see if it's true.

Endnotes

[1] See 2 Sam. 6:17

[2] See Eph. 1:3 (you have everything), 2 Peter 1:3 (you have everything), Col. 2:8-10 (you have the entirety of God living in you, which means you don't have to spend your life seeking "more.")

[3] G5248, Strong's Concordance

[4] G5228, Strong's Concordance

[5] G4052, Strong's Concordance

[6] Definition taken from Free Dictionary

[7] Taken from Thesaurus.com

CHAPTER 2

The Problem with "Grace"

Here is one of the major problems we have in the church: we sing songs with lyrics like "if grace is an ocean, we're all sinking," but whenever a drop of that ocean's grace applies to anyone outside of our churches in a way that isn't accompanied by a religious agenda to convert them to our belief systems, we immediately get uptight and offended, want to pull in the reins on grace, and accuse people of not taking sin seriously. Then we create labels that make grace exclusive to those who meet our conditions, and demonize anyone who actually demonstrates it as the unconditional thing it is.

Instead of showing the world the love and kindness of Christ (the same kind He showed us), we tell them they better quit doing what they're doing or this wonderful Bridegroom is going to toss them onto His bar-b-q during the wedding party. We think it's *our* job to convict the world regarding sin when scripture says that job belongs to the Holy Spirit. But whenever people don't go out and aggressively rub sin in people's faces, an angry mob forms to say, "They're saying sin is okay!" No. We're just choosing to believe that God can do His part of the job ("convict the world regarding sin") better than we could, and that the message He has entrusted to us is that He isn't holding their sin against them. (2 Cor. 5:20)

God's Mercy on The Worst of Sinners

Why did God have mercy on Paul, the "worst of sinners"?

> *"...so that in me, the worst of sinners, Christ Jesus might display his immense patience as an example for those who would believe in him and receive eternal life." 1 Timothy -1:16 (NIV)*

Because Paul was the "worst," He was the perfect person for God to display His mercy through, in order to show every other "sinner" in the world that He's not angry and wanting to kill people over sin. If He were as angry and vengeful as so much of the church makes Him seem, then He surely would have destroyed the "worst of sinners" (along with a nearby city) to show all the other sinners in the world how much He just can't put up with sin; but that's not what He did. He had mercy on the "worst" to show His patience for the rest.

Does this mean He enjoyed the idea that Paul took part in murdering His people? Does this mean He was "endorsing" Paul's sin or saying, "You're free to run around and do that as much as you'd like!" No. That's such a senseless conclusion to come to! But Paul says in Romans 7 that the Law was the problem because more Law equals more sin. Had God only pushed the Law on Paul and tried to force him to change his naughty behavior, Paul's persecution addiction would have become much worse. Instead God showed kindness and grace, and it was that kindness and grace that turned Saul into Paul through a changed perspective of his father.

This was the revelation Paul received from Jesus and continued to preach for His whole life. According to Saul's beliefs as "a Pharisee of Pharisees," God wanted to destroy the sinners and blasphemers (that's why he was persecuting the church), but all of the sudden he found himself to be the worst of sinners and blasphemers, and instead of finding God's harsh judgment and need for revenge, he found God's kindness and mercy. This ruined everything he thought he knew about God. No longer did he see a destroyer of nations, but a lover of the creation. Not just a lover of people who think they are doing right by defending God's Laws (like he was doing), but also a lover of "sinners" who do really dumb things out of ignorance (like he was doing)—even a lover of Pharisees (*Gasp!*). God loves the best like He loves the worst—Paul was both, and his story is a testimony of God's extreme grace.

False Grace

So then ask yourself what the "false grace" message really is. Is it the kind of grace that abounds over sin and displays Christ's immense patience for all (the kind that changes hearts forever, instead of temporarily changing behavior)? Or is the "false grace" message the kind of grace that desperately tries to mix in with the Law and as a result creates a "loving God" who loves people as long as they agree with Him, but otherwise throws temper-tantrums and destroys cities and nations? Which kind of grace did Paul give testimony about in his letter to Timothy? (1 Timothy 1:12-17)

Grace means "undeserved kindness," not "deserved wrath." Yet, many who oppose "hyper-grace" and claim to know the *real* meaning of grace won't hesitate to say that God is angry at people over their sin, and He must seek justice (which is usually just a code word for revenge). If that's what *real* grace is, then it's no wonder those outside of the church want none of it. That's not grace, that's murder. And unfortunately for the Christian image, the guy supposedly responsible for this graceful murder is the same one who said, "You shall not murder." And His Son, who is the perfect representation of the Father said to "love your enemies" not "destroy them." Don't we have a word for those who don't practice what they preach? Those outside of the church do!

He's God of All

One of the things Paul dealt with in the book of Romans was the Jewish idea of exclusivism. Read it from front to back and you'll see that Paul is trying to tell his audience that God isn't only the God of the Jews, but the God of the Gentiles as well. He's not an exclusive God that only belongs to one elite group over another (those with the perfect theology and behavior), but the God of all.

The Pharisees thought He was exclusive, and that they should be the sole beneficiaries of His grace, and that's one of the many things that ticked them off about Jesus. He brought God to the outside of the exclusive club (to Samaritans, Canaanites, Gentiles, etc.), down to the street trash and city scum (lepers, tax collectors and harlots) where the religious leaders didn't think God belonged, because He's so holy and offended by sin. But He is the God of the dirty as much as the clean; the unholy as much as the holy; the unrighteous as much as the righteous; nobody is on the outside.

Is that a scary thought that He belongs to everyone? Only if you take the approach that they don't deserve it because they don't believe like you, keep the rules you keep, or repent like you repent. That's the same mindset the Pharisees had. Why are you still making it about you and what you do, or them and what they do? Why are you more concerned with rule-keeping than with the well-being of people and the "free gift" God wants to give them?

The Gospel is the happy news that "God was in Christ reconciling *the world* to Himself, **not** holding their sin against them."[1] Whose sin is He not holding against them? **THE WORLD.**

Does this mean everyone is reconciled, righteous, and saved? Although that's a common fear for people who oppose this message, no, it doesn't mean that at all. As much as I desire to be reconciled to my church friends who left me over this message, I can't be reconciled to them without them wanting to be reconciled to me as well. I can send emails and make phone calls, but if there's no desire on their end, they're not going to respond. It doesn't help that some of them think I'm an anti-church, Christian-hating heretic, who has betrayed their congregation and gone off the deep end. Why *would* they return my messages if they view me through such a negative lens? And if God is presented as a murderous madman dangling people over Hell by their ankles so they'll "repent" and reluctantly "love" Him, or wiping out entire cities because of a disagreement with a political issue, who really wants to return His emails besides the few who fall for His manipulative fear-tactics?

The Good News of Fear and Judgment

Although we say "there is no fear in love," we also try to coerce people into loving God through a fear of Hell and judgment. It's hypocrisy. It's not grace. We may spiritualize it to the point of believability among ourselves, but the unchurched see right through it, which is why they stay far from it.

This message of absolute grace and forgiveness is supposed to be the point where Christians celebrate, not get grumpy and argue for reasons why God has to exclude certain people (or murder them). Do we even think about these things? Why do we speak of God and Heaven as if He's looking for more excuses to keep people *out* than

He is to let them in? How silly do we make Him sound when we call Him "unconditionally loving" and "full of grace," but then find all kinds of conditions for why He can't treat people like He loves them?

It's not about forcing people to change their beliefs and actions through fear, but helping them change their perspective of God through love and kindness; to understand that He's happy, not angry—He's not holding their sin against them. Does it mean He likes when they sin? No. But He is patient with them despite their sin in the hopes that they will see His kindness and repent.

> "Instead he is patient with you, not wanting anyone to perish, but everyone to come to repentance." – 2 Peter 3:9 (NIV)

"Well, you know, brother, 9/11 was the result of homosexuality in our country, and God had to judge America!"

No. "He doesn't want *anyone* to perish." How many people perished on 9/11? Enough to say it wasn't Him who wanted it.

When people have a proper perspective of their creator, and they know He's not a short-tempered, genocidal crazy person, they will be able to "boldly approach" Him like the people did with Jesus. They came to Him on their own, not through the force and obligation of fear. They didn't run to Christ because He scared the hell into them, but because He took the hell *out* of them.

Freedom from Sin

The grace message, which is now being ignorantly slandered around the world, is the invitation to the whole creation to boldly approach their creator without the fear that He's going to crush them because of their rotten behavior. Come and meet your Creator and find out how graceful and loving He really is. Don't cower down in fear, He's not out to get you. Why? Because you deserve this kindness? No. That's why it's called grace.

The message is not "go around and keep sinning because God is such a nice guy!" but rather, "Christ has come to deliver you out of that perpetual life of doom and depression that none of us want to be a part of, but we also don't know how to get out of on our own. He has removed the thing causing that vicious cycle of sin. Now you are free to live and enjoy life without the constant feeling of guilt and shame over behavior you don't know how to stop doing, and the fear that God is going to destroy you over it."

God is not an angry dictator.

What is the opposite we've been taught? "Quit sinning because God is angry! He will punish sinners and drive them away! Christ has come to forgive our sin, but we're always going to sin because we're so wicked!"

Really? That's what we've labeled "good news" and "grace" in Christianity? Let's get real.

Tell me which message is the one actually giving people permission to sin: the one that says, "You're free from sin! You don't have to live that way anymore!" or the one that says, "You're prone to sin as long as you live! But you better try your damned hardest to avoid it or God is going to judge you!"

Why This Message is Offensive

The real deception about grace is coming from these fear-based rumors that are filling websites and magazines with religious propaganda, teaching people that God cares more about the rules than He does about you, and that anybody who emphasizes His love for you more than His love for rules is somehow saying it's okay to break the rules.

How is a kindness earned through rule-keeping called "grace," when the definition of grace means kindness is unearned?

The people teaching these things are only doing so because they fear that if rules aren't emphasized, then control will be lost and anarchy will erupt. None of us want anarchy, but scripture says very clear that Lawlessness gets its power from the Law (2 Cor. 15:56). I'm glad these leaders don't want anarchy and they want to keep people from sinning, but they're the ones perpetuating sin by enforcing a Law that was given to increase it (Romans 5:20).

The grace of God *is hyper* (highly excited, extremely active), but it's extremely offensive to those whose ministries revolve around the idea of an angry and vengeful God punishing cities and nations over sin, where their Romans 5:20 sounds more like "... where sin abounds, God gets really angry and kills a lot of people." That's not what it says.[2]

Fear is the motivator behind those kinds of messages because fear is great at keeping the sheep in line and under control. It's great at making people feel secure without having to deal with the inevitable messes caused by giving people freedom to learn by their mistakes. If the followers lose their fear, then the leaders lose their means of influence, since their influence is based on how much they can use fear to get the desired behavior from their followers.

If someone can make you think that a "great deception" lurks outside the walls of their ministry then you will forever stay contained within, quenching any curiosity and questions you may have about a world outside. Welcome to the matrix, where you are now locked inside their system, and every action and thought you make is orchestrated by them. You're convinced that you're helpless against deception on your own, so you need to go to their conferences, buy their books and DVDs, and subscribe to their prophetic words in order to stay out of deception. They never teach you how to stay out of it on your own, they just tell you what it is and to stay far away from it.

It's the same fear that caused the Pharisees to murder the Son of God and anyone who dared to speak His name. The crowds lost interest in ideas about God that were based on fear because Jesus brought a new idea about God that was based on His kindness and love, in which there is no fear.[3] Jesus didn't go around picking on sinners and telling them to quit sinning "because the Ten Commandments say so!" He hung out with them in their houses and taught about God's kingdom. As a result of Jesus' message and demonstration of "unearned kindness," the Pharisees began losing their influence, because their influence was entirely based on how much they could coerce people to do religious jumping jacks through fear of God and guilt of sin.

If your business consists of putting a carrot on a stick and having people pay you for the opportunity to chase it, then it's no good for your business when a group of people comes along and starts giving away carrots for free. Yet, this is what we see in the life of Jesus and His disciples. The Pharisees demanded a proper performance from the people before they were worthy of God's mercy (as many ministries continue to do today), but Jesus poured out mercy and forgiveness freely and without condition. He didn't say, "go and sin no more, and then I won't condemn you!" He said, "I don't condemn you, go and sin no more!"

The grace message is not that God doesn't find a problem with sin, it's that He found such a HUGE problem with sin that He sent His Son to destroy it and remove it from our lives forever.[4] Sin isn't the issue anymore. More often the issue is the believer's perspective whenever they live as if He didn't deal with sin, thinking they are still "prone" to it when Paul said to "consider yourselves dead to it."[5] For the unbeliever the issue is often the image that they've been presented about God. They can't help but perceive Him as a hostile maniac because that's what the Church has made Him look like through their endless threats of judgment and terror in the name of "unconditional love" and "grace."

Perception is the problem, and both believers and non-believers need a better one of God, themselves, and each other. And this is what Jesus did. He brought a better perspective of God and humanity. But like today, it was only the religious, the Law-obsessed people who were unwilling to change their perspective and accept that God wanted to extend grace and kindness to those outside of the temple club. For as much as they were focused on getting everyone else to repent, they were never willing to do it themselves.

Though many love to throw the word "grace" around, the idea of God's kindness is still a huge problem for those who need Him to be angry in order to coerce their congregations into better moral performance, and to scare those on the outside of the church into becoming members as quickly as possible. Sure, He's nice when you live up to His standards, but as soon as you don't, He's an entirely different person who goes on a rampage. Somehow that gets called "unconditional love," when it isn't anything close.

> *"Some people need a theology of an angry God to justify their anger against sinners." – Bill Johnson*[6]

This grace message is biblical if you would just look into it without your preconceived ideas of what it's saying. It has received the same reactions from those obsessed with Laws since the days of Jesus, where the people who emphasize the Law go into a panic and think that if the Law isn't preached, people will act crazy and do whatever they want. This is what they thought about Jesus, it's what they thought about Paul, and yet we can look at both of their lives in scripture and see that none of these fears were ever valid, because neither of them were ever telling people to sin; instead they were empowering people to live free from sin through a demonstration of God's kindness and grace.

The only ones Jesus and Paul harshly rebuked were the religious Law-keepers who were desperately trying to drag God's children back into the efforts of Law-keeping that leads to death.

Endnotes

[1] See 2 Cor. 5:19, this is the message He has entrusted to us!

[2] Definition taken from Merriam-Webster.com

[3] See 1 John 4:17

[4] See 1 John 3:8

[5] See Rom. 6:11

[6] Taken from Bill Johnson's Twitter

CHAPTER 3

Are You Saying
All Sins Are Forgiven?

Besides thinking we're telling everyone to indulge in sin, one of the major problems opponents of "hyper-grace" have is the idea that God has forgiven all sins, past, present and future. Simply looking up the definition of forgiveness has helped me a lot with this.

Forgive:[1]

1. To excuse for a fault or an offense; pardon.

2. To renounce anger or resentment against.

3. To absolve from payment of (a debt, for example).

We Have to Ask for Forgiveness!

For the sake of the argument, let's say that people are right when they say that Jesus' sacrifice wasn't for complete forgiveness (past, present and future), and it was only to forgive past sins and provide us with the ability to *ask* for our future sins to be forgiven. Going by the definition above, that would mean that *until I ask*, God is consciously choosing to hold my faults and offenses against me, consciously choosing to be angry and resentful towards me, and consciously expecting payment from me for my sin (on top of what Christ already paid).

These implications make it clear why so many God-loving Christians have such a hard time boldly approaching God's throne like they're His children. They constantly expect to run into an angry Dad who is consciously resenting them because of their behavior (behavior they're told they will continue doing until they die. Adam and Eve had this same skewed view of God; it's what caused them to hide in fig leaves. But the idea didn't come from God, it came as a result of eating from the wrong tree.

Do you think that your Father is blatantly ignoring the payment of debt that Jesus made on behalf of the entire world regarding sin? That's doubtful. Yet when people insist that forgiveness only comes through asking, they are putting conditions on a gift that was meant to be unconditional through the sacrifice of Christ.

If we aren't forgiven until we do something for it (ask or confess), then we're earning that forgiveness, which takes grace (undeserved kindness) out of the picture and says we must meet a certain standard before we deserve it. Then it's no longer a "free gift," it has now become "wages."

> *"And since it is through God's kindness, then it is not by their good works. For in that case, God's grace would not be what it really is—free and undeserved." – Romans 11:6 (NLT)*

Are You Saying We Don't Need to Confess Our Sins?

Is confession unnecessary then? Many opponents of "hyper-grace" will claim that this is what the "grace camp" believes. Personally I've still found use for confession, if for nothing else it keeps me humble by admitting my mess-ups. Confession has been an amazing thing in my Christian journey and the more benefits I see coming from it, the less I hesitate to do it. However, continuous confession isn't necessary to receive continuous forgiveness (or in other words, God only forgives the sins you confess and ask Him to forgive, but not the ones you miss).

Don't throw the book down yet! Hear me out.

If God isn't holding my sin against me (and according to 2 Cor. 5:19, He's not), then by definition I'm already forgiven. Personally, I confess my sins because I've found it beneficial to my personal growth. I'm not doing it to get something from God, I'm doing it to keep myself in a position of humility, not trying to hide my mistakes or sweep them under the carpet of denial or shame, but admitting them so I can position myself to learn from them and grow in wisdom. I run to God and say, "This is what I did. I shouldn't have done it. What's the source of the problem?" I'm not confessing in order to receive forgiveness or beg for mercy, but in order to take a knee in humility and receive teaching from my Father.

Am I worried about a rule? No. I'm focused on Jesus and who He is in me. I want my life to reflect Him more and more. If He wouldn't do it, I don't want to do it either. I'm not avoiding it because I want to keep a rule and avoid God's anger, but because I want to enjoy communion with Him as He lives through me. I've learned to let my sin strengthen communion with my Father, not destroy it. That doesn't mean I'm willingly running around sinning so I can have better relationship, it just means that if I do become aware of a sin, I immediately take it to Him as an opportunity to learn, instead of trying to hide it from Him in shame, thinking He is sitting on His throne with His arms cross and His foot tapping.

My overall focus isn't on sin, it's on Him. I'm not on a witch-hunt for sin (not mine or anyone else's), and I'm not focusing on ancient Laws that are impossible to live up to. I'm enjoying this relationship and the fact that He is already pleased with me, not because of my actions but because of my identity.

Confession is a good thing, but it's not the currency with which you buy forgiveness from your Father. I'm not doing it to coerce God into forgiving my sins, I'm doing it to humbly acknowledge, "I don't know what I'm doing here, but I recognize there's a problem, can you teach me the solution?" And what does He do? He teaches me! Why? Because that's what good fathers do!

As far as anti-confession teachings being popular in the "grace camp," They're not. That's simply another myth people have made up about the "hyper-grace" movement, created by those who hope to bury it for the sake of their traditions. I think we in this "movement" only have a different perspective of how confession works and what it's for. We're not trying to get anything out of God that He hasn't already given, we're merely enjoying the benefits of the uncorrupted relationship we have with God in Christ. So then we're not approaching God as timid servants in fear of our master, but as confident sons in love with our Father.

"What about 1 John 1:9?"

I've already written an entire chapter on 1 John in my book, *How to Overcome Sin*, so I'm not going to go into great detail about it again here (lest all my books be repeats of the other!). But 1 John 1 wasn't written to believers, it was written to the Gnostics.

He isn't telling the Gnostics (or the believers) they must continue to confess each and every one of their sins to receive forgiveness, he's telling them to confess that their sin exists (because Gnostics believed that sin was an illusion), so they can experience the reality of His forgiveness and be purified from unrighteousness.

How can you experience the benefits of forgiveness and righteousness if you don't think there's anything to be forgiven for and purified from? The word "confess" there means to agree, and not to deny. Since the Gnostics denied that they had sin, they also denied that they had done anything that needed forgiveness. How can you share in the benefits of Christ's cross and the forgiveness of sins (or in John's words "have fellowship with us") if you don't think there is anything to be forgiven for?

The very observant ones will have noticed I said, "...experience the benefits of forgiveness" above, implying that they were already forgiven. What makes me think such heresy? Because remember what Paul said, "God was in Christ, not holding men's sin against them." If you're not holding a person's offenses against them, then by definition, you have already forgiven them (not to mention the numerous other verses throughout scripture that says He has taken away the sins of the world).

> "You're saying the whole world is forgiven and saved and going to heaven! *Blasphemer!*"

No. Before you tear your robe, look at what I said. Yes, I believe the whole world is forgiven, in that God is not holding their sin against them—scripture says this clearly—but the whole world hasn't received this forgiveness either (just like the Gnostics didn't). That means they aren't experiencing the benefits of that forgiveness (fellowship with Christ, being purified from all unrighteousness, and too much more to list!).

It doesn't matter how much I forgive you, if you don't believe I've forgiven you, or you stubbornly insist that you've never done anything offensive that needs to be forgiven, then you're not going to enter into fellowship with me and accept what I'm offering. Forgiveness would be worthless to you if you think you don't need it. Likewise, if you think you've never sinned, then the gift of being forgiven and purified from all unrighteousness would be just as worthless. This is what the Gnostics were doing. They didn't believe sin was real, so forgiveness and purification of sin was of no use to them (or so they believed!).

John is telling these Gnostics, "Quit saying you don't have sin. If you believe that then you're calling God a liar, you're deceived, you're walking in darkness, and the truth is not in you! Instead, confess your sin (acknowledge it, quit denying it), receive His forgiveness, be purified from unrighteousness, and have fellowship with us!"

John isn't telling Christians they need to confess every sin in order for that sin to be forgiven (can you imagine how many missed sins would be piling up and waiting for you on Judgment Day?). He is telling non-Christians (whose teachings were creeping into the church) to stop playing make-believe and stop denying the gifts of God by thinking you don't need what He's giving away.

As a believer you are forgiven and purified of *all* unrighteousness. Does anything about that verse imply that you ever become unforgiven and unrighteous the next time you sin, and therefore you need to be forgiven and purified all over again? No. So then why do we use that one verse as a basis to say we need to continuously confess our sin in order to be continuously forgiven and purified? It never says that—it doesn't even imply it.

The Unforgiving Wife

In a Facebook video with Sid Roth, Dr. Brown attempts to build the case that not all of our sins are forgiven, but only our past sins are.[2] He uses the example of his marriage and says that because he's in a relationship with his wife, whenever he sins against her he has to ask her for forgiveness. I understand what he might be trying to say, but I think he's confusing forgiveness with a good old-fashioned apology.

As I mentioned before, the automatic implication of this logic is that until he asks for forgiveness, she's consciously holding that sin against him, and she's consciously choosing to be angry and resentful towards him over whatever he has done to offend her. Now when you phrase it like that, I doubt Dr. Brown would say that's what his wife is doing, because those are obviously not the signs of a healthy relationship, and that would make her sound rather *graceless* in the attempt to defend "true grace." However, given the definition of forgiveness, that's what's implied, whether it's intentional or not.

That kind of treatment doesn't make for a healthy relationship, because every time you screw up you immediately expect that person to be consciously and purposefully angry and resentful towards you until you ask them not to be. This would make it very awkward and hard to approach that person when you expect that sort of reaction from them all the time. After a while you start to walk on eggshells around them because you don't know what's going to set them off and what isn't. It doesn't make you want to get close to them, it makes you want to stay out of their way. Any little thing you do to tick them off is going to result in you being made to feel like the most inferior scumbag in the world, as they purposefully separate themselves from you to rub it in your face and guilt trip you into "repenting."

Unfortunately, that's how a lot of Christians relate to their heavenly Father; I used to relate to Him that way as well. It really didn't make me want to get closer to Him, it made me want to avoid Him altogether because I hated the constant knot in my stomach whenever I was around Him. It didn't mean I didn't love Him, but because I was always terrified and constantly anticipating judgment from disappointing Him, I didn't enjoy being around Him. I was like Adam after he sinned, all I wanted to do was hide in the darkness to avoid letting God see my shame (thinking He was just going to lecture me and make it worse). Yes, I sang and danced to all the happy songs, cried through all the sad songs, and told God how much I loved Him, but inside I was terrified of constantly being rejected by Him because I kept offending Him with my sin.

I don't know Dr. Brown or his wife, or how their marriage works, but if they're a happily married couple, I doubt she's walking around consciously holding his wrongdoing against him (and I doubt he's holding hers against her). And if she's not holding his wrongdoing against him, then by definition he's already forgiven. He might apologize and say, "I'm sorry I hurt you," but as far as forgiveness is concerned, it's already done. She chooses to forgive on her own without him having to ask. They're in a relationship, and in a healthy relationship you don't walk around consciously angry and resentful at the person you love, holding their wrong against them until they ask you not to. "Love keeps no record of wrongs."

When I first heard the grace message, I found out that I didn't need to hide from God, because He wasn't showing up to shame me, He was showing up to remove my shame. He did this in the Garden with Adam, but because Adam was so focused on the sin and shame, he was ignorant of God's intentions and resisted Him. Even still, God clothed them as a way to take their focus off of their nakedness (the cause of their shame).

This is the heart of our Father. He isn't showing up to rub sin in our face so we feel guilty and beg for mercy, but to take our focus off of shame so we can continue in pure relationship with Him. In forgiving our sin and promising never to remember it, He has made the declaration that He isn't focused on our sin, and we shouldn't be focused on it either.

When Are We Forgiven?

The argument Dr. Brown makes is that God has only forgiven past sins, and future sins are only forgiven if you meet the requirement of "asking." In other words, God has already given us a head start on forgiveness through the cross, but it's up to us to keep the forgiveness train moving.

One thing worth remembering is that God isn't contained inside this capsule of time and space like we are. There's no such thing as "past, present, and future," to Him—everything either is, or isn't.

"Jesus Christ is the same, yesterday, today, and forever" (Heb. 13:8).

How can that be? Because He's inside yesterday, today, and forever all at the same time.

"Christ is all and in all" (Col. 3:11)

"He is before all things, and in him all things hold together." (Col. 1:17)

"Before Abraham, I am" (John 8:58).

"The lamb that was slain before the foundation of the world." (Rev. 13:8)

He exists—not just past, present or future, but always. He is. He's not contained within this ever-expanding box we like to call the universe, and therefore He isn't limited by its Laws. Whether those be the Laws of time and space as we see in the verses above, the

Laws of gravity as we see when He walked on water and ascended into the sky, or the Laws of life and death as we see in His resurrection.

The problem, especially with people stirring up this "hyper-grace" controversy, is that they've added limitations where He has added none, and they have kept limitations where He has completely removed them.

> "But Christ offered only one sacrifice for sins, and that sacrifice is good for all time. Then he sat down at the right side of God. And now Christ waits there for his enemies to be put under his power. With one sacrifice Christ made his people perfect forever. They are the ones who are being made holy. The Holy Spirit also tells us about this. First he says, 'This is the agreement I will make with my people in the future, says the Lord. I will put my Laws in their hearts. I will write my Laws in their minds.' Then he says, 'I will forget their sins and never again remember the evil they have done.' And after everything is forgiven, there is no more need for a sacrifice to pay for sins." – Heb. 10:12-18 (ERV)

He offered one sacrifice, good for *all time*, not just one time. The Greek word for "all time" there means "continuously," which means "uninterrupted in time."[3] The writer of Hebrews isn't saying that Jesus is continuously making sacrifices for sins, but that the effects of His *one* sacrifice are uninterrupted—continuously good.

He did this, not because we asked for it, but because we were in need of it. Love doesn't have to wait to be offended before it moves forward in forgiveness, and neither does it need you to give it permission to forgive. You can try to say that it's relational and if you offend your wife you have to ask for forgiveness, but again, that implies that your wife is purposely holding your sin against you, and she will continue to do so until you ask her to forgive you. It's conditional love and forgiveness, and that's not the kind Jesus displayed.

Love doesn't let anything bring separation between it and the object of its affection. If I have to wait for you to ask me for forgiveness before I can forgive you, that means I'm willing to hold your sin against you until you prove to me how sorry you are and ask me to stop being angry. I'm purposefully holding a barrier between us and dangling your sin over your head and saying, "if you ever want me to let you close again, you first have to meet this requirement!"

How many of you husbands treat your wives that way? How many of you fathers treat your children that way? Yes, there's still discipline and consequence for disobedience, but you're not consciously resentful towards your wives and children until they ask you not to be, and you're surely not going to destroy a small city because they don't listen to you. That's the *opposite* of grace; grace doesn't wait for you to deserve it, it says, "Here I am because you don't deserve me, but I love you anyway!"

Scripture says that "God was in Christ, not holding people's sin against them." (2 Cor. 5:19) He said, "I will forgive their wickedness, and I will never again remember their sins" (Heb. 8:12). How can He be holding something against someone or feeling angry and resentful about something that He doesn't even remember?

Are You a Better Forgiver Than God?

Why do we have no problem saying things like, "I choose to forgive this person. I'm not going to let their behavior ruin my day!" and yet when it comes to God's forgiveness we say, "He can only forgive you if you ask!"? Why do you have the ability to forgive people unconditionally (without them having to ask or beg for it), but God only has the ability to forgive people on the condition that they ask and show how bad they feel?

If you step on my toe, then before you ever even apologize I can choose not to get angry at you over it. But with God, if you step on

His toe, He immediately becomes furious, and the only way to calm Him down is to ask Him not to hold it against you. If this is true, then no matter how much you spiritualize it, His ability to forgive is inferior to our own. How likely do you think that is?

If you hurt me, I can forgive you and there's nothing you can do about it because it's not your choice whether I forgive or not, it's mine, and only mine. You can get mad at me and say, "I don't want your forgiveness!" or do what the Gnostics did and say, "I haven't done anything that needs to be forgiven!" But you can never change the fact that me forgiving you is entirely my choice to make, and you have no say in the matter. I forgive because I want to, not because I have to.

Jesus Forgave People Before They Asked

How much asking and begging was required by the adulteress in John 8:11 before Jesus chose to forgive her sin? She never confessed or asked Him anything, yet He chose to let her off the hook and not hold her sin against her.

Jesus said, "I do not condemn you." Compare that with the definitions of "forgive." It means, "I'm not holding this thing against you. I'm not angry or resentful towards you over what you did." Then what? "Go and sin no more." Why? Because it's that unconditional love and undeserved display of trust and kindness that empowers the person to leave their life of sin. "Why would you let me off the hook when I deserve to be punished?" Isn't that how most of us started following Jesus? Not because we were scared of hell, but because we encountered the love of this person who refused to hold our rotten behavior against us when everyone else did.

We wander from our first love, not when we forsake His Laws (which are Laws the Bible says we're no longer even under), but when we forsake His kindness, because it was His kindness that wooed us in the first place.

> "Or do you presume on the riches of his kindness and forbearance and patience, not knowing that God's kindness is meant to lead you to repentance?" – Romans 2:4 (ESV)

The Paralyzed Man (Luke 5:20)

The interesting thing with this story is, not only is the man not coming to Jesus for forgiveness (he's coming for healing), and not only does he never ask for forgiveness or confess his sins, but Jesus declares the man's sins forgiven after seeing the faith of the *man's friends.*

This ticked a bunch of people off, because their perception for how forgiveness of sins works was like many today: "You have to do something to receive it. You need to sacrifice an animal and cry at an altar and show God just how guilty you feel over your badness before He can forgive you!" But Jesus comes along and addresses forgiveness when none of the people are even consciously looking for it.

The Jewish people had yearly sin offerings where they would sacrifice their pets and ask God to forgive them and remove their guilt. So when somebody came along with the nerve to not only forgive sins, but to do so without there first being some kind of ritual offering or condition met, they got offended because it made all of their works and rituals look pointless.

The Woman and the Perfume (Luke 7:36)

What about the woman in Luke 7 who poured perfume on the feet of Jesus? Again, without her asking or confessing, He says, "Your sins are forgiven," and again, people got upset. He then goes on to say the famous line about whoever is forgiven much loves much, and whoever is forgiven little loves little. Do you notice that the forgiveness comes before the love (or in Paul's terms, the kindness comes before the repentance)?

All through the Old Testament when the prophets prophesied of the Messiah, it came along with numerous promises of how God wasn't going to count their trespasses against them. This woman believed it and her response was an incredible show of love for her Messiah. She showed her love for Him because she was first loved by Him, not to coerce Him into loving her.[4]

The Thief (Luke 23:43)

How about the thief on the cross? The thief makes a confession about Jesus being an innocent man, and asks Jesus to remember him when He goes into His kingdom, but he never asks for forgiveness. And even though Jesus doesn't say "Your sins are forgiven" as directly as he did with the paralyzed man and the woman with the perfume, by definition He forgives the man by choosing not to hold his sin against him.

Everyone Else (Luke 23:34)

Perhaps the most famous example of this is when Jesus was on the cross. They have shown Him no mercy or remorse for what they've done. They've stripped his clothes and gambled for the pieces, and while they're in the middle of mocking Him and saying, "If you're really the Son of God, take yourself down from there," He responds and says, "Forgive them, Father. They don't know what they're doing."

And God responded and said, "No! They haven't asked!"

No, that's not what happened!

Those people didn't ask for His forgiveness, and they probably weren't even aware of needing it, nor did they care about receiving it. Yet, Jesus, who said, "If you've seen me you've seen the Father," chose to forgive the very ones who were killing Him, without them ever meeting the conditions we put on forgiveness today.

This should be amazing news that makes us excited to wake up every day and go tell the world. Not news that gets us worked up and makes us demonize people for daring to believe God is really this good. Or makes you get angry at me because I'm taking away your right to go yell at sinners when you were once in their shoes and God "didn't treat you as your sins deserved."[5]

Is Asking For Forgiveness Wrong?

Can you ask for forgiveness? Of course! But why is it necessary to ask for something you already have? If I do or say something stupid, of course I say sorry, but I don't ask Him to forgive me when I know He already has. Instead I say, "Thank you that you've already forgiven me, and you're not holding it against me!" That may sound like a trivial difference, but it's actually a big deal. It changes your entire perspective and the way you relate to Him. It's a huge difference from, "I'm so sorry! I'm so unworthy! I can't do anything right! Please don't hold that against me or lift your hand of Grace from me!" (I used to pray that way!).

Instead of approaching His throne like a worm in fear of being crushed, you learn to approach Him confidently and full of thankfulness. Not "Thank you for not killing me!" but "Thank you for not letting this affect our friendship." You love much because you know you've been forgiven much; you're not loving much in the desperate hopes of convincing Him to forgive much.

Asking for forgiveness isn't "wrong" per se, but it also isn't necessary, and it teaches you to stay conscious of your sin instead of conscious of His grace and kindness. If He's not remembering your sin anymore, why are you?

Your sins, past, present and future are forgiven (which includes being forgotten). Not because you did anything to earn that forgiveness, but because He did (before the foundation of the world). He has willingly chosen to forgive you, not because you ask, but because He loves you and isn't letting the relationship hang on the hinges of your behavior.

He's not holding your sins against you, not even the ones you don't ask Him to forgive. If anyone would say different, I have one question: *where did Jesus ever do that?* Jesus told his disciples that the only way people weren't forgiven is if the disciples chose not to forgive them.[6] And if you're choosing not to forgive people, you've missed the heart of God displayed clearly in the life of Jesus.

Endnotes

[1] Definition taken from <u>Free Dictionary</u>.

[2] <u>Has God Forgiven Our Future Sins?</u> (From Sid Roth's Facebook page.)

[3] <u>G1336</u>, Strong's Concordance, Definition taken from <u>Free Dictionary</u>

[4] See 1 John 4:19

[5] See Psalm 103:10-11

[6] John 20:23

CHAPTER 4

Are You Saying Repentance Isn't Necessary?

Yet another assumption opponents of "hyper-grace" make is that we are saying repentance isn't necessary, or that it's only an old covenant thing. Not to throw a wrench in the works, but I repent frequently, and I know some other "hyper-grace" teachers do as well. However, my interpretation of repentance isn't groveling at the feet of Jesus, shedding tears at an altar, or feeling guilty over bad things I do. It's "renewing my mind," and bringing it (or rather, asking Him to bring it) into a proper alignment with who He is and who I am.

The word repent in the Greek (as used in the New Testament) means to change the way you think—change your mind. What does "change your mind" mean? You used to think one way, but now you think another. A lot of people's repentance is powerless because they think repentance means to cry and feel sad a lot, but since they never actually change their mind about the things that make them sad, they're never empowered to quit repeating the same problems over and over.

"God, I'm just a horrible sinner!"

Okay, well what are you going to do about it?

"I'm going to confess to God how sinful I am and ask for His mercy!"

He already showed you His mercy and took away your sin. So, again, what are you going to do about it?

"I'm going to confess how much of a sinner I am!"

Then expect to continue sinning. If you think you're full of sin, don't be surprised that your life is overflowing with it. You don't fill a cup with water and get surprised and disappointed when the water runs over the sides do you? So if you think you're full of sin, why are you surprised that sin is overflowing from your life? Change your perspective. Scripture says you're holy, righteous, and perfect.[1]

"Nobody is perfect!"

Stop. Are you going to cling to that self-righteous attitude, thinking your self-abuse shows God how humble you are, or are you going to "repent" (change your mind) and believe what scripture says about you? "Nobody is perfect" might be a nice little Christian saying, but it's not in scripture. Hebrews says that His sacrifice has perfected you *forever.*

Do you act like it all the time? No way! Neither do I. But I'm closer than I was than when I used to confess was how sinful and imperfect I was, thinking I was being spiritual when all it is is false-humility.

We always say, "We live by faith, not by sight." Then why are all of our confessions directly related to what we see? "I sin, therefore I'm a sinner!" Okay, well then don't be surprised if you continue seeing sin in your life, since you're basing the future of your life on what you see. That's not repentance. Faith moves mountains it doesn't declare them as mountains—that's just stating the obvious, which takes no faith. Stop declaring what *you* see and start declaring what *He* sees. Change your perspective.

That's a practical look at how true repentance works. It's not shameful to cry and feel sad, but it doesn't matter how much you do that if you're not changing how you think.

When a baby is learning to walk, they fall. The reason they eventually stop falling is because every time they fall they change their mind based on what made them fall. They may not realize that's what they're doing, and we may not realize what they're doing (and the few who have said repentance isn't necessary may not realize that they do it every day), but when you make a mistake, you examine what went wrong and correct for the next time. This is all repentance is—it doesn't need to be any more complicated, "deep," or "spiritual" than that.

When I was a teenager and I used to skateboard, and I fell quite often. But every time I fell, I examined what made me fall, and I made sure to fix it next time. "My feet were too close together and my knees were too stiff, which made the skateboard fly out from underneath me when I landed on it. Mental note: Next time I land, spread my feet further apart on the board to keep my weight more evenly distributed, and bend my knees to absorb the impact." What did I just do? I repented—I changed my mind. I used to think one way (which resulted in falling), now I think another, and the fruit of my repentance shows in my ability to stand on a skateboard without falling down.

In that sense, I repent all day long about numerous things, not only things that apply to Christianity. However, I don't cry and beat myself up over those things; I give myself grace and understand that I'm learning.

The Repentance Gimmick

Is repentance an old covenant thing that's obsolete? No. It's an everyday part of life. However, the popular interpretation of repentance (which is really no repentance at all), meaning to cry at an altar and make self-sacrifices for your sin and guilt (or for the sin of your nation), is an old covenant thing, and it doesn't help anything.

Firstly, you can't repent for the sins of the nation, because by definition that implies you can change your mind for them. What makes any of us think we can do that? You can cry and feel bad for the sins of your nation, or fill expensive stadiums with tears and groaning, but there's a reason that has gone on endlessly year after year with no tangible results: it doesn't work, because it isn't true repentance. It's the same thing Jesus told us not to do: standing in public and praying to show everyone how devoted to God we are.[2]

One of the problems all Christians succumb to is the thinking that growing numbers are a sign of a successful ministry. And since millions have joined the popular prayer/repentance movement of today, it's automatically assumed to be a success. But abortion is still legal, homosexuality is making more progress towards becoming legal every day, and all of the things that so much time is spent "repenting" about are either continuing to go on, or getting worse.

True repentance in this case would be to admit that those tactics for change aren't working, and to start trying something else. But that hasn't happened, which makes it a safe conclusion to say that the people organizing these things year after year don't really understand what repentance is, since by definition they are unwilling to *change their mind.*

I don't say that with the intention to insult anyone or put them down, neither do I say it to cast judgment on the intention of their heart. I'm 100% sure they are genuine about what they are doing, and they work with all of their passion and effort to organize those things. Their work is appreciated. But the reality is that what they are doing hasn't worked, and they keep trying to do the same thing anyway.

If repentance means to change your mind, and you spend 30 years doing the same thing over and over, not only are you unrepentant by the Biblical definition, you are also *insane* by Albert Einstein's.

> *"Insanity: doing the same thing over and over again and expecting different results."*

Today's popular interpretation of repentance isn't biblically accurate, and it doesn't fix anything. That's where many in the "grace movement" seem to have a problem. Their problem is not with repentance itself, but with the popular definition we've been spoon-fed for our entire Christian lives; a repentance more focused on sadness and guilt than it is on the action of change.

If you look at the repetitive conferences and prophetic words that go on year after year, they don't ever bring about any lasting change (if any at all), which keeps every promise on the horizon but never makes it a reality for the people pursuing it. If that large portion of the church would truly "repent" (by the Biblical definition of the word), then they would see all the things they've been praying for and predicting for years and years.

I might even dare to ask the question, what if this "grace movement" is a result of their years of prayer, but like the Pharisees did to Jesus, they're attempting to kill the thing they've been waiting for because it didn't come in the way they expected it to? The Pharisees thought the Messiah would come and reinforce their traditions, but instead He came and challenged them. What did they do? They built up all kinds of false accusations against Him so they could write Him off and continue along with their traditions uninterrupted, even though what they were doing never actually brought any change. What was the result for them? They missed the thing they were spending all of their time praying for because no matter how much they talked about loving God, they loved their traditions more. It would be wise then, for the opponents of "hyper-grace" to make sure they're not making the same mistake: praying for a move of God and then crucifying it when it comes.

True Repentance

If repentance doesn't result in a change of action, then it isn't true repentance. If you spend ten years repenting for the same action you've been doing the same way for that ten years, you're not really repenting. Repentance at least makes you screw up a little differently each time, since you're changing your mind and how you do things. I'm not saying that to shame anyone who has been stuck in the same sin for ten years, I'm only saying that if you ever want to be unstuck, you need to change how you think about the problem, not just cry and feel guilty over it.

I used to be a compulsive manipulator with severe anger problems. I "repented" all the time (meaning I cried and felt guilty over it), but I also thought I was a "sinner" who was doomed and damned to act that way all my life because my heart was wicked. I thought, "This is just *my* sin. Some people are addicted to alcohol... some are compulsive liars... I'm just an angry person. That's how I am!" The church did nothing but fuel the fire of that belief by telling me it was my nature to sin, and that my heart was wicked and deceitful. It wasn't until I heard the grace message and found out that Christ removed sin from me and made me into a new creation (meaning all of the old has passed away), that I was finally set free from a lifetime of anger and temper-tantrums (and the guilt and depression that followed every fit of rage). I stopped believing I was just an angry person when I started believing I truly was a new creation.

Do I still get angry and frustrated at times? Yeah. But I don't break other people's things or go on a 5-minute long rampage in the process, blacking-out and destroying anything that isn't nailed down. When I started to believe that I wasn't that person, I stopped being ruled by the compulsions that ruled that person. I "repented." I renewed my mind and stopped believing it was my nature to be an angry person. I stopped believing that I would always ruin all of my relationships through manipulation and guilt-trips. I quit crying and feeling guilty about the problem, and I changed how I perceived it by actually daring to believe the good news that Christ has set me free by forgiving *all* my sins, and making me brand new in Him.

I stopped just quoting the scriptures and singing the songs, and I actually dared to believe. So much that I started declaring myself *already* holy, righteous and perfect, and I quit trying to make myself into something He already made me into. "I'm not a sinner, I'm a saint! Don't you dare tell me different because you're lying if you say so! Scripture declares me *righteous* and I don't care what you say, or what I feel, or what I act, I'm sticking to it!"

My Perfect Theology

I'm not against repentance at all. In fact, without it I might just be dead (and happy about it!). I'm thankful for repentance, and it continues to make my life better every day. But I understand now that repentance is far different than what I was commonly taught by the modern church. As a result, I've stopped repenting the "popular" way since it only made my problems worse. Now I actually stay humble so I can truly repent by changing my mind and learning from my mistakes.

This is something we all need to keep in mind, not only those in the "prayer movement," but those in the "grace movement," as well. The moment we settle for our current belief systems is the real moment repentance becomes unnecessary because we feel there's nothing else we need to change our minds about. We become unwilling to change because we've concluded that we already have everything figured out and our theology is perfect.

Had I stubbornly insisted that the grace message is *only* freedom from sin, which is how I was introduced to it, then I would have never been empowered to heal the sick, or realized that everything I was begging God for in revival had already been given through His son. I would still be chasing the celebrity Christian leaders around, trying to get an anointing from them, when the Anointed One lives in me and I'm already anointed by Him.

Yet, even though I've learned those things, I'm *still* learning new things about this gospel. I've learned to keep an open mind so I can continue to grow and learn. But here's the catch, I only keep an open mind about good news, since that is the definition of the word "gospel." For many, this becomes reason to slander us and the grace message, by saying things like, "If it's not good or doesn't tickle the ear, they just ignore that it's in scripture!" No. I'm not looking to have my ears tickled, but I am "testing everything and holding onto what is *good* (not bad)." I don't settle for "bad news" because the gospel is good news. It's not "partially good news but mostly bad news," it's good news through and through. I'm looking for news that will set me and other people free, not drag us back into the hell of Law-keeping, or spiritualized hopelessness. If you want to live your life that way, that's your choice, but I already lived mine that way and I will never return.

Is my current theology the "best," then? No. But it's better than what it was when I was giving all of my efforts to something I already had all along. It's better than it was when I thought I was in the "desert place," separated from Christ because of my sinful behavior (which I thought was my nature), and completely unaware that Christ has already brought me into the Promised Land. It's better than it was when I was hopelessly trying to purge sin from my life while being taught I was stuck in a sinful body with no chance to ever really live free from it until I died.

I can critique those ideas and their outcomes with accuracy since I've actually believed those things and have been down those roads. Yet, most who are criticizing this "hyper-grace" movement have never given it a chance, so their opinions can only be assumptions and paranoia based on what they *think* the negative results of it are going to be (ignorant of what the positive results have already been for countless people).

I've already played the "revival" game and found out it doesn't work (as many others in the "grace movement" have), so I won't be going back to it (I've "repented"). I keep moving forward and discovering new things, testing everything to see what works and what doesn't, holding on to whatever works and is proven good, and getting rid of everything else. Repentance isn't a once a week thing, or a once a year thing when it's the theme of the big conference.

Repentance never ceases. I don't have set schedules for repentance; I repent every time I recognize a need to learn something new.

Obligatory Disclaimer

Please don't misunderstand the above as slander against the prayer-movement. I only wish to point out that the same thing has gone on in that movement for over a decade (the same yearly prophetic words and promises of revival and a "new thing"), but no matter how hard they have pressed in and pursued those promises, the "new thing" remains "on the horizon" and "around the corner" year after year. People are made to believe that it's their fault and they just need to pray harder and pursue more passionately and live more pure. That's not repentance.

I was once a part of all of that, and I believed those same ideas. But when I first heard this gospel of grace, I learned that God has already provided everything I spent so much time laboring to get from Him. It's only through rest and acknowledgement of the work Christ has already accomplished that those things move from "on the horizon" and come within reach. When you quit trying to get God to provide a "new thing" and accept that He has already provided everything you will ever need through His son, then your stressful labor will cease and you will enjoy the benefits of the promises you've been pursuing. That's when you will enter the rest it talks about in Hebrews 4.

This is the area where the charismatic church needs to repent. Stop doing the same things over and over and expecting different results—stop repackaging the same conferences, books and vague prophetic words and trying to pass them off as something "new." Instead start preaching the Gospel that Christ has already given us everything we need—this is the only gospel there is.

We don't need to "be filled," we already are. We don't need to "pursue God," He has already pursued us. We aren't trying to call Him down out of Heaven through our good works and displays of devotion, but He has already come down on His own because of His grace. We are already one with Him.[3]

Endnotes

[1] See Heb. 10:10, 10:14, 2 Cor. 5:21
[2] See Matt. 6:5
[3] See Eph. 1:3, 2 Peter 1:3, Col. 2:10, 1 Cor. 6:17

CHAPTER 5

Are You Saying
We Can Sin All We Want?

If you get pulled over for speeding and the cop doesn't give you a ticket, is that cop telling you that it's okay to speed? No. His choosing not to hold your wrong against you is not an invitation to go and do that wrong again. This accusation that "hyper-grace" preachers are giving people a "license to sin" is just simply stupid (I'm sorry, but there's no better word for it!). It's not logical, it makes no sense, and there's no actual evidence for it anywhere. When has anyone in the history of the world ever needed a license to sin anyway?

When Rick Joyner and Bill Johnson publicly showed grace to Todd Bentley after his fall in 2009, were they saying, "Great job, Todd! Go and do that sin again!" No. They were very open about how what he did wasn't okay, but they chose to have grace on him anyway. It was called "Todd's restoration." And even though many other leaders in different denominations took the opportunity to load their shotguns and call for Todd's public execution from ministry (and all the humiliation that comes with it), Rick, Bill, and others in the Charismatic movement sacrificed their own reputations to stand between him and the wolves who were just looking for a feast. Again, were they endorsing his sin? Or merely showing him grace despite his sin?

In the same way, I don't endorse sin, and neither do any of the "hyper-grace" preachers. But we have grace for those who do sin because we understand that we're all growing and maturing into the full stature of Christ. We believe that it's grace, not Law that brings restoration, just as Rick and Bill believed with Todd.

The only difference between us and our accusers is that we don't only limit that grace to those in our own "camp," we believe it applies to the whole world (not just in theory, but in practice). If I'm going to show grace to Todd, I'm going to show it the same way to everyone else, because Todd is no higher on the pedestal than anyone else in the world.

Why We Don't Preach the Law

Although nobody in the grace movement is saying grace is a license to sin (nor have they ever), it's often assumed that, since we don't emphasize the Law and push it on people like our accusers think we should, we must be endorsing sin and telling people it's okay to do whatever they want. In truth, we avoid pushing the Law because we believe what scripture says about the Law. That the Law increases sin (Romans 5:20), sin gets its strength from the Law (1 Cor. 15:56), the Law is the ministry of death (2 Cor. 3:6), the Law isn't based on faith (Gal. 3:12), and nobody can be made right with God through keeping the Law (Gal. 2:20). In fact, though many preachers will tell us today that it's sin that separates us from God, and we need to go back to His holy Law to be reconciled, scripture actually teaches the opposite. It says that the Law is what separates people from Christ and causes them to fall from grace (Gal. 5:4).

Our choice to not enforce those Laws is not because we want to see people sin, but because we want them to live free from sin. Scripture is very clear that those Laws are the very thing causing people to sin. While we receive many accusations that our grace-emphasized message is a "license to sin," if you look at the church today, and all throughout its entire history, sin and the blatant abuse of people has always been done in the name of the Law, not in the name of grace. Nobody has ever killed anyone in the name of God's grace, and yet countless crusades and wars have been waged in the name of upholding and enforcing those Laws. Why do we ignore what scripture so clearly says about the law? "The letter kills..."

Sin finds its strength in the Law—it reproduces itself through the Law. While the Law itself is good, it's also vulnerable. This is why we don't focus on the Law, we focus on the grace and kindness of God that leads men to repentance and teaches us to say "no!" to ungodliness.[1]

Those in the "hyper-grace" camp don't despise the Law, and we acknowledge what Paul said in Romans 7:12, that the Law is "holy, righteous, and good." The Law has a proper place, but that proper place is not in the life of believers (1 Timothy 1:9). Yet, even when being preached to unbelievers, the Law is not meant to threaten them with judgment and death for disobedience, or to try and coerce them to live up to those standards. The Law is meant to show them that they could never obey it, no matter how hard they try.

The Law is meant to crush you. It is meant to make you miserable. It is meant to destroy your entire life until you finally give up on your obsessive need to perform and say, "God, help me! I can't do this!" Because at that point, when faith in yourself has finally come to its end, the only person left to put faith in is Jesus.

The Law is not meant to be kept, it's meant to kill every ounce of hope you have in trying to keep it.

We think when Jesus said, "You have heard it said do not commit adultery, but if you even think about it you're guilty," that He was trying to get them to be more obedient to those Laws. He made those Laws impossible. He did it on purpose so they would *stop* trying to live up to them and put their faith in Him. He wasn't trying to rally them up for holiness when He said, "If your right hand causes you to sin, cut it off!" He was telling them how severe the Law really is if they were going to continue trying to live by it, because they had cheapened it and made it doable just like so many have today. Jesus was saying, "You want to gain holiness and purity that way? Cut off your hand and gouge out your eye if they cause you to sin. Because if you break even one of those Laws, you will be judged for breaking them all."[2]

Contrary to the accusations our accusers make about us ignoring the words of Jesus, cut off your hand and gouge out your eye was *not* a metaphor. It was the unsettling reality of the lengths a person has to go to if they hope to keep the Law. He was saying it in the context of lust. So think about what He means when He says, "gouge out your eye." Why? So then you won't look at women that way. Cut off your hand. Why? Think about it. He was telling them that it was a heart issue, not an issue of bad behavior. But if you want to just focus on the behavior without dealing with the heart, then those are the measures you will have to take in order to keep your behavior in check. His plan was better, "Let's deal with the heart, and the behavior will change by itself."

Look at the example of the Rich Young Ruler.

> "Jesus. I've kept all of the commands, ever since I was a child. What else do I need to do to gain eternal life?"

How does Jesus respond? "Oh? You think eternal life comes through your effort to please God by your performance? Sell everything you have, give all of the profit to the poor, abandon everything you've worked your entire life to gain, and follow me. Then you will have eternal life."

He couldn't do it. His entire life was based on his work and what he did to earn riches (whether material or spiritual), and Jesus said, "Leave it all behind. Follow me. Then you will have what you're looking for."[3]

It's time for you to make the same choice: will you continue trying to please God and gain spiritual riches (holiness, righteousness and purity) by what you do? Or will you leave all of that behind and *really* follow Jesus by putting your faith in Him and accepting the holiness, righteousness and purity that only comes through what He did?

The choice is yours. I'm only here to show you the options.

***

I don't look at a growing child and expect them to act like an expert adult. I give them grace when they mess up because I know that messing up is part of life and learning. The moment I put limits on someone's ability to mess up, I put limits on their ability to learn, which in turn limits their ability to grow. I'm obviously not going to encourage anyone to go out and purposefully mess-up so they can learn a great life lesson, and indeed, there are still consequences for messing up, but that's why we have a Comforter. If a person does mess-up, I show them grace and kindness because it's His kindness that leads to repentance. I comfort them and strengthen them through encouragement and reassurance in how great they are. "I'm here for you. I'm not going to abandon you over this. We'll figure this one out together. I've got your back!" I don't belittle them and tear down their character, thinking my harsh treatment will guilt-trip them into acting better. What nonsense!

If someone can't have grace for people despite their sin (Christian or not), and they are more concerned with abusing a long list of rules to control people's behavior (most of which are rules they don't even keep themselves), then they have missed the very basics of the Gospel. If the "grace" includes threats of judgment and punishment, or a manipulative pressure to coerce you into acting a certain way, it's not from God and you have permission to ignore it. That's false grace.

"How can you make such a claim?"

Because "God is love," and

> *"There is no fear in love. But perfect love drives out fear, because fear has to do with punishment." – 1 John 4:18 (NIV)*

You do not have permission to sin—

"Wait. Did you just say we should go sin?"

No. Once again, loud and clear:

You **DO NOT** have permission to sin.

Jesus has taken away every excuse you have to continue sinning. But you are growing up into that knowledge and learning more about the freedom He has brought us through the cross, so you do have permission to learn from your mistakes apart from the constant fear that He's wants to kill you over them. His grace gives us room to breathe while we learn, without the fear that He's waiting for us to screw up so He can "convict" us and make us feel like horrible people.

I'm not choosing not to sin so I can keep a rule and avoid God's judgment and wrath, I'm choosing not to do it because grace has taught me to say "No!" to ungodliness, and His kindness (refusal to judge me by my bad behavior) inspires me to want to live a better life (a life free from sin). It's the love (not the fear) of Christ (or hell) that compels us.[4] I'm not motivated by the fear of breaking rules. I'm motivated by the love and grace that has freed me from that unbearable obligation.

✳✳✳

Let me say it one last time for those who are still asking the same question.

"Does this mean we can go out and sin?"

No. It will never mean you can go out and sin. It will always mean that you don't need to hide from your Father if you do sin, because His grace and kindness (not anger and disappointment) is meant to lead you to repentance (a change of mind, which leads to a change of heart, which leads to a change of action). More importantly, this grace has set you completely *free* from sin. We're no longer waiting until we die to be free from sin, instead we are considering ourselves already "dead to sin, but alive to God in Christ."

The message of grace being preached is not that you should abuse God's kindness, but that you should enjoy it apart from the fear that He wants to destroy the world because of sin.

I would sum up the message of grace as "the message of reconciliation" in 2 Cor. 5:19. That God was in Christ, bringing the cosmos (the entire universe) back into favor (reconciliation) with Himself, not holding men's sin against them. This is the message He has entrusted to His followers.[5] The message is not that God was in Christ judging the world and destroying men because of their sin, but that God was in Christ, not holding their sin against them.

This is the good news that God is happy, and it's a dangerous doctrine to those who need Him to be angry so their ministries can stay afloat, and their rulebooks can still hold appeal. Abandon that old rusted ship! Jump overboard into His love, and let yourself sink into the ocean we call His grace!

Endnotes

[1] See Rom. 2:4, Titus 2:11-12
[2] See Gal. 3:10
[3] See Mark 10:17-27
[4] See 2 Cor. 5:14
[5] See 2 Cor. 5:19-20

Concluding Remarks

Always question every person that expects you to behave right, but never gives you room to grow through making mistakes.

Always question every person that forbids you from asking questions. If they're desperately trying to cover something up or get you to shut up about it, let it peak your curiosity, not snuff it. Let it make you wonder what it is they're trying to keep from you. No matter how unbiblical they say it is for you to question them, or how "submissive" and "honoring" they demand you to be.

Never let your questions be silenced. When you lose your voice you lose your freedom.

Scripture tells us to, "Test everything and hold on to what is good." It never says, "Take everybody's word for everything and only hold on to what they give you permission to hold on to." Don't let any leader pull the "submission" card, or the "Don't touch the Lord's anointed" card in order to coerce you into blind and silent obedience. Jesus never did that. He's the guy who said, "Ask and you will receive."

Never let anyone convince you that God considers it "doubt," "disloyalty" or "dishonor" if you question Him, or the leaders He has put into leadership positions. Jesus welcomed and encouraged questions of all kinds (that's how people learn!).

Never let anyone convince you that faith means to quit asking questions in favor of silent obedience to your leaders. Not only is that a lie, but it's also blatant manipulation and behavior control. The only ones who have done that kind of thing throughout history are cult leaders and tyrants who were afraid their followers would learn to think for themselves. Because a single question can be the most powerful weapon against fear and tyranny, and one question has the power to topple an entire empire.

Don't ever underestimate the power of a question.

Your questions are the greatest weapon you have against deception, manipulation and tyranny; never let anyone disarm you.

If your leaders are trying to teach you to fear them, it's time to find new leaders. The only reason they would want you to fear them is so you will do whatever they say without asking questions. That's not the church or Christianity that Jesus founded—that's something else entirely.

Don't let your leaders disguise fear as "respect" or "honor." There is a huge difference. Respect and honor is something you give naturally, not something you have to be coerced and guilt-tripped into giving reluctantly.

Always line everything up with the person of Jesus. You didn't become a Christian to follow me or any other church leader; you became a Christian to follow Christ. If something doesn't line up with Him and what His life demonstrated for us (that is, those in the new covenant), you can safely conclude that it's no good. And if it's tested and found no good, you will know not to hold on to it. (I've written an entire book about this subject called *It's All About Jesus*.)

If you find what I say is good (by measuring it up to Jesus), great! Hold on to it. But if it isn't (because it doesn't line up with Jesus), I won't be offended or disheartened if you reject it. I like you way more than I like my opinions and perspectives of scripture (no matter how right I think some of them are). I'd rather you be well off and enjoying life in the Spirit than holding on to some stupid opinion of mine in the flesh for the sake of "loyalty." Being loyal to me as a person doesn't mean you have to be loyal to all of my ideas—that goes for every other church leader as well. If they mistake disagreement with disloyalty, then they have an ego problem. Don't let them try to bully you into thinking you're the problem for not agreeing with them.

Don't mistake good intentions for infallibility.

Finally, don't settle for doctrines that diminish how much you are loved.

To read more work by the author, you can check out his blog SaintsNotSinners.org, where you will find many encouraging articles to help you experience true freedom. If you are interested in finding out more about Hyper-Grace, you can find more resources at *Hyper-Grace.com*.

Other Books by D. R. Silva

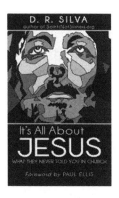

IT'S ALL ABOUT JESUS:
WHAT THEY NEVER TOLD YOU IN CHURCH

D. R. Silva challenges the biggest giants of modern church doctrine to see if they measure up next to the life of Jesus. This book will reveal the source of most problems in the Christian life and will show you how to find the quickest solution.

Is it God's will to heal everyone? Are you destined to sin until you die? Was Jesus sacrifice only for forgiveness of sins and heaven when you die? This book looks past all of the superficial catch phrases, spiritual hype, and countless excuses that have kept Christians powerless for years. It examines every question in the light of the life of Jesus, and the answers you find will shock and amaze you!

"D. R. Silva's book, *It's All About Jesus*, is one of several refreshingly honest Christian books I've read lately. He is open about the process he's gone through in transitioning from what much of modern Christianity teaches, to a more authentic relationship with God in Christ."
– **Joshua Greeson**, author of *God's Will is Always Healing*

"This book will help those who are newer to the faith avoid some of the pitfalls the rest of us went through in the Christian walk."
– **Steve Bremner**, SteveBremner.com

"I wish more people would ask the sorts of questions D. R. Silva raises in this book for they are questions that illuminate and liberate. And they are questions that will lead you to a deeper revelation of the greatest Answer of all."
– **Paul Ellis**, author of *The Gospel in Twenty Questions*;

EscapeToReality.org

How to Overcome Sin:
A Practical Guide to Freedom

Are you ready to uncover the secret to living sin free?

Continuing his trend of putting popular religious traditions under the microscope, D. R. Silva takes on one of the most important topics in all of Christianity today: sin.

Have you ever wondered if it was possible to live completely sin free? Do you want to know how sin functions so you can avoid it effortlessly? Are you tired of the same old religious formulas and programs that never deliver on their promises to help you live holy?

D. R. Silva knows how you feel, and the answers he has found are simpler than you've ever dreamed!

D. R. Silva is part of an exciting breed of young authors proclaiming the gospel of radical grace. Unafraid to ask the big questions or confront manmade traditions, he writes so that the church might live up to its full potential in Christ. *How to Overcome Sin* is a book that will challenge the way you think and help you to see your life through the awesome work of the cross.

—**Paul Ellis**, author of *The Hyper-Grace Gospel*

D.R. Silva is a great author who navigates the reader around the potholes of religion and leads them into the safe fields of grace.

- **Mick Mooney**, author of *SNAP*

This book is a refreshing change, bringing a truth that will be water to your soul - Jesus has made you righteous and completely set you free from sin!

– **Phil Drysdale**, PhilDrysdale.com

ABOUT THE AUTHOR

D. R. Silva is a Best Selling author and compulsive question asker. His blog, SaintsNotSinners.org, has inspired tens of thousands of people around the world. Together, his highly acclaimed books, *It's All About Jesus: What They Never Told You in Church* and *Hyper-Grace: The Dangerous Doctrine of a Happy God* have helped set countless people free from bondage to legalistic religion. He is best known for his conversational writing style and frequent use of parables that make complex topics easy to understand. The goal of all of His writing is to point everything to Jesus.

Made in the USA
Middletown, DE
30 September 2015